sarah walker

ELECTRONIC KEYBOARD BASICS 2

CD edition

to all my students at Longford Community School

© 1998 by Faber Music Ltd
First published in 1998 by Faber Music Ltd
3 Queen Square London WC1N 3AU
Cover design by Russell Stretten
Design by Susan Clarke
Illustrations by Drew Hillier
Music processed by Wessex Music Services
CD recorded by John Whiting
Printed in England by Halstan & Co Ltd
All rights reserved

ISBN 0 571 51833 8

FABER *ff* MUSIC

Contents

CD Contents ⓒ1

The disc contains performances of the pieces, exercises and group activities in the book so you can hear how they sound; the interactive tracks (marked with an asterisk) also give you the opportunity to play along. Simply turn down one of the balance channels on your CD machine or amplifier and play the missing part. There is either a count-in or a short rhythmic introduction to help you begin on time.

* = Interactive track

Introduction

Electronic Keyboard Basics 2 is the perfect musical companion for the keyboard student who is no longer a beginner. Using a multitude of fun, accessible pieces, the book introduces bass-clef reading, key signatures and scales. Confidence with counting is encouraged through special 'Drumkit dynamo' exercises, and ear training continues through 'Echo playing' and improvisation. *Electronic Keyboard Basics 2* also aims to develop the student's ability to play for others; there are special sections on performance, articulation and building a repertoire, and many well-known tunes are featured, including the ever-popular theme from *The Snowman*.

Both volumes of *Electronic Keyboard Basics* are suitable for any type of electronic keyboard and contain plenty of useful hints for individual and group lessons. Beginning at a level equivalent to Trinity College's 'Initial' grade, this book progresses to beyond Grade 1.

Dynamics are left to the player's discretion, as they will depend largely upon the environment – a small, quiet practice room will call for a softer level than a busy classroom.

unit 1 Not one clef, but two!

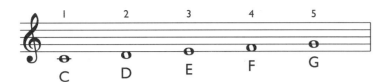

Recognise this? It's a <u>treble clef</u>, followed by the notes of the C major 5-finger position you learned in Book 1.

Now have a look at this:

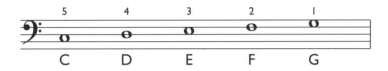

This is a <u>bass clef</u>, along with the same five notes. But this time, they're an octave lower: the same note-names but eight notes lower.

The bass clef is used to write out, or notate, low notes. On the keyboard, you normally play low notes with your left hand.

So left hand isn't just for playing <u>auto-accompaniments</u>?

NO, a competent keyboard player can read symbols <u>and</u> bass clef notation. Read on . . .

Bass clef solo melodies

These tunes use three notes only:

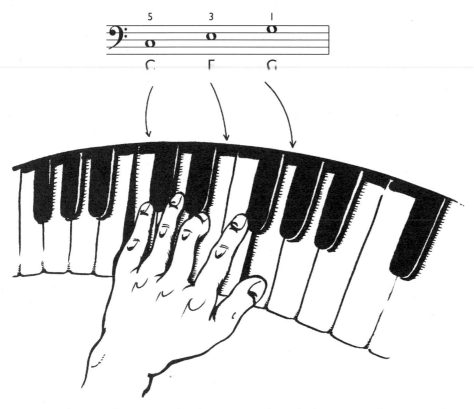

As you're not playing autochords here, make sure the auto-accompaniment function is switched off.

Simple solo CD 2

voice: strings

Strict solo

voice: trombone

Smart solo

voice: electric guitar

Now try playing C, E and G together:

That's a C major chord. You can get the same effect by switching to auto-accompaniment, or bass chord hold, and pressing a low C.

Bass clef melodies using the C major chord

Military melody ⓒ 3

voice: accordion

Mellow melody

voice: piano

Mighty melody

voice: harpsichord

More bass clef notes

Left-hand march CD 4

voice: piano

Left-hand waltz

voice: strings

Left-hand melody

voice: trombone

Hands together!

In the next two pieces, left and right hands play together in octaves: the same note-names but 8 notes (one octave) apart. Practise hands separately.

Octave march no. 1 ⓒ 5

voice: horn

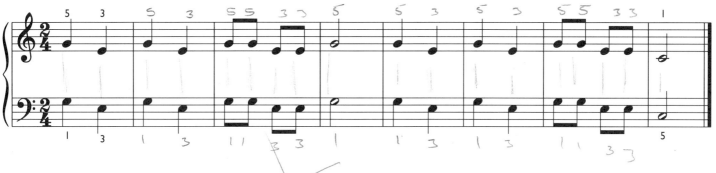

Octave march no. 2

voice: trumpet

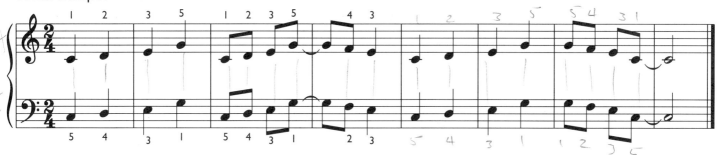

Did you manage the syncopated rhythm OK?

Clap and count:

one and two and (one) and two

Heroic hymn ⓒ 6

voice: strings

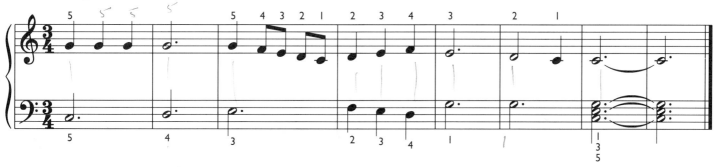

Moon dance © 7

Practise the left-hand part separately – notice how little finger holds on to C for the whole bar, while thumb and 2nd finger keep moving. Think of your little finger as an anchor!

voice: fantasy

Moderato ♩=144

Ternary form

All through the history of western music, composers have written pieces in a structure called **ternary form**. They begin with a theme (A), then progress to a contrasting middle section (B), before returning once more to the opening theme (A). Did you notice that **Moon dance** uses this form?

GROUPS Divide into melody players and accompanists. If you have more than one instrument, use a different voice on each. Experiment to find the best combinations!

Now you know about:

- The bass clef
- Playing a C major chord
- Ternary form

unit 2 C major...and its relative minor

This is a scale of C major. You can tell it's a major scale when you listen, because it has a special pattern of **tones** (T) and **semitones** (ST) – steps and half-steps.

To play a C major scale, you just play all the white keys from C up to the C above.

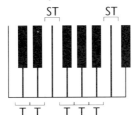

A semitone is the smallest interval, or gap between notes, that you can play on a keyboard.
A tone is two semitones, the next smallest interval!

You've already played the first five notes of the C major scale, but if you want to go all the way to the top, you'll have to use some new fingering! Try this:

tuck thumb under 3rd finger

Once you've put your thumb on F, the rest is easy.

Now try playing up and down the scale:

thumb under

3rd finger over thumb

Try to join the notes up smoothly – the musical term for this is *legato*.

Solo melodies using the scale of C major

Merry melody CD 8

voice: alto sax

Muted melody

voice: flute

Marching melody

voice: piano

GROUPS Once you've learned the melodies, try playing them together in different registers (high, middle and low), using a variety of different voices. One instrument should provide the beat, which could increase in speed each time through.

Drumkit dynamo no. 1   CD 9

Introducing semiquavers or sixteenth notes!

There are four of these in the time of one crotchet.

count: one – i – and – a   two – i – and – a   three – i – and – a   four – i – and – a

For these exercises, choose two percussion sounds – a high one
(perhaps a cymbal) and a low one. Use finger 2 of each hand.

Dotted notes

When you see a dot after a note, add on half of the
note's value: ♩. = ♩ + ♪

Try these dotted rhythms.

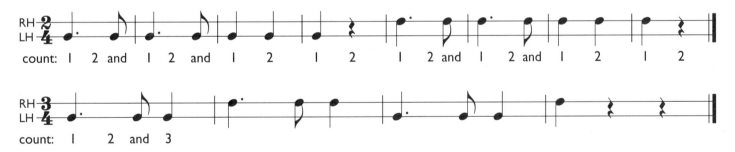

You could write out the last two exercises using ties.
Try them again – they sound just the same!

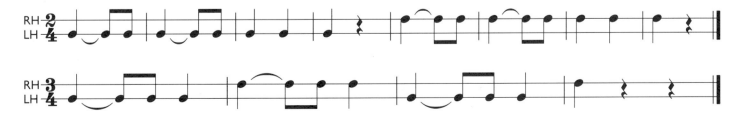

Dozing dinosaur ⓒ 10

The dotted left-hand notes represent the heart-beat of a lightly sleeping Tyrannosaurus Rex – *disturb at your peril!*

* If you find the semiquavers (sixteenth note) chords difficult, don't worry: the struggle adds to the drama!

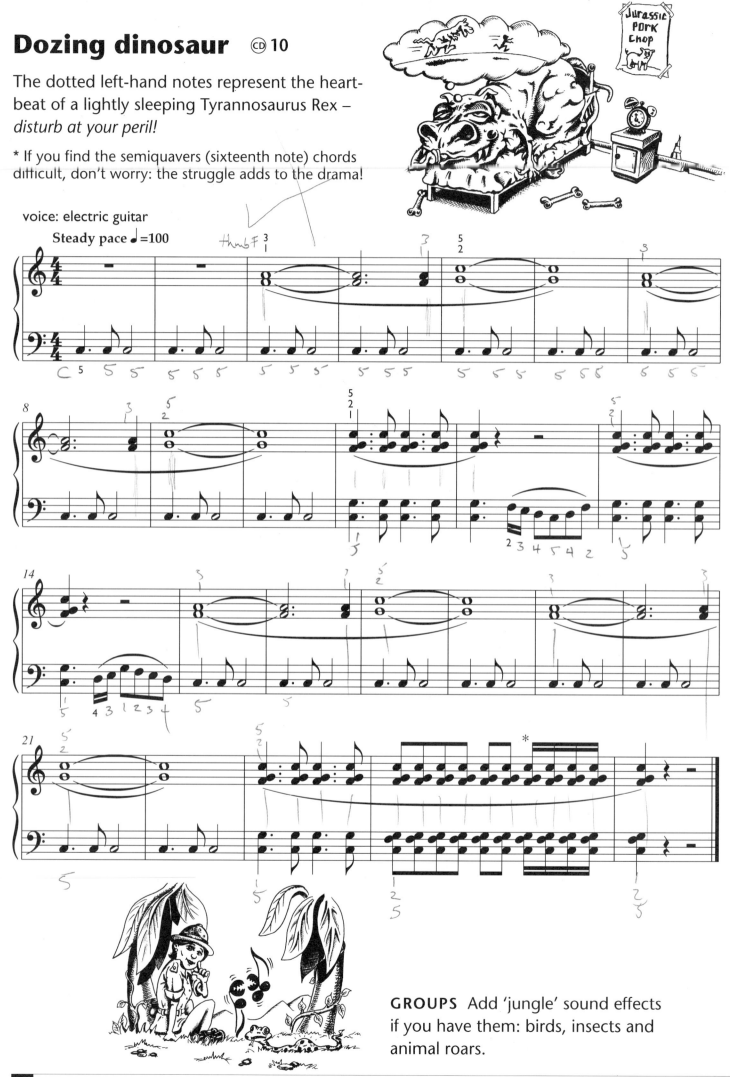

GROUPS Add 'jungle' sound effects if you have them: birds, insects and animal roars.

Three useful chords in C major

Three of the most useful chords in any key are the ones built on the first (I), fourth (IV) and fifth (V) notes of the scale. In C major these chords are C, F and G. The following traditional tunes use these chords.

Transpose these pieces up an octave if middle C is in the auto-accompaniment range of your keyboard.

This note is B below middle C

Did you notice how neither of these pieces started on the first beat of the bar? The note, or notes, which lead into the first beat are called an <u>upbeat</u>.

Sumer is icumen in

This piece is a round: it was written around 1250 and is one of the earliest surviving pieces of secular (non-religious) music. A round is a melody made up of short, even sections. At the start of each section, a new player enters, and as each one reaches the end of the tune they start again. This can go on for ever!

Version one: for groups (CD) 13

Each player must learn the melody carefully. Player 1 starts; when he or she reaches the point marked *, player 2 enters, and so on. Keep repeating the tune as many times as you like.

GROUPS One player should provide a drone to be held throughout the performance. Try playing C and G together, using a sustained voice such as electronic organ. The drone could start first, allowing player 1 to enter in their own time.

Version 2: for solo players CD 14

These exercises will help you with the bass clef part:

voice: electric organ

Allegretto ♩.=92

Allegretto means fairly lively.

Scaling the heights CD 15

Spend plenty of time getting to know the melody and the chord changes before you put the two together. When you do try playing it with both hands, use 'bass chord hold' before you add a rhythmic style. Remember to start slowly when you play with a rhythmic accompaniment – listen carefully to the strong beats so that you keep in time.

voice: tenor saxophone
style: 8-beat

Con brio ♩=112

GROUPS While one student plays the right-hand melody, another could play autochords (firstly without an accompanying rhythmic style, then using an '8-beat' or similar style). A third student could play the melody in a different register, using a contrasting voice.

Relative minor

Every major key has a **relative minor** – a minor key which has the same number of sharps or flats in its key signature. The relative minor of C major is A minor; neither has any sharps or flats. Minor keys often sound more mysterious than major ones! On the next page there are two versions of a well-known traditional tune in A minor.

New notes E, G, A

The house of the rising sun: version 1 ⏺ CD 16

voice: electric organ
style: rock 'n' roll/rock shuffle

Steady pace ♩=112

Traditional

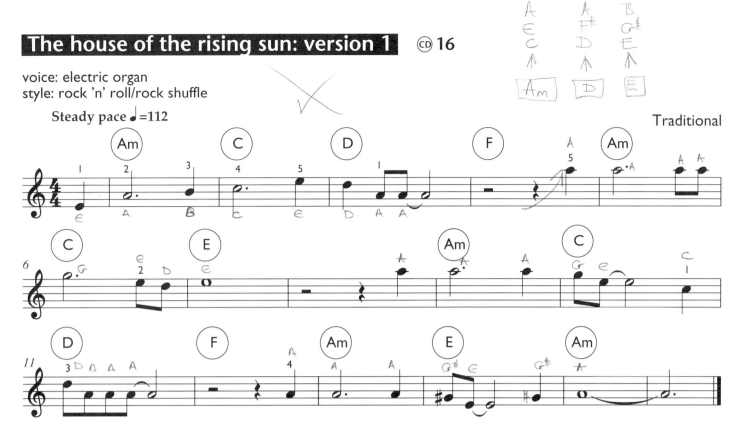

The house of the rising sun: version 2 ⏺ CD 17

voice: electric organ
style: rock-a-ballad

Fairly slow ♩.=69

Traditional

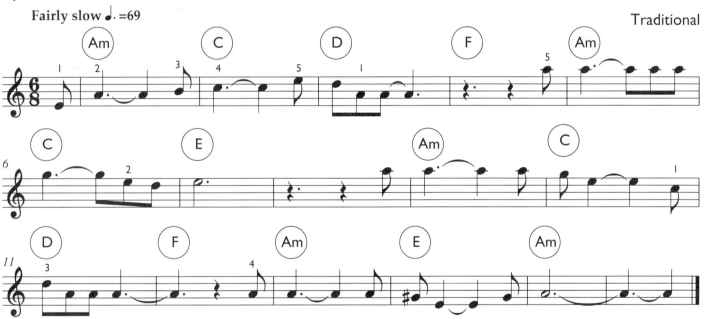

Can you tell the difference between these two versions? The first is simpler, in 4/4 time, and goes with the funky pre-programmed song that some keyboards have (look in the 'song' section of the keyboard). Version 2 is a 6/8 version which is more similar to the 1960s hit single.

Now you know about:

• Tones and semitones
• C major and its scale
• Semiquavers (sixteenth notes)
• Dotted notes
• Chords I, IV & V
• Upbeats
• A minor

unit 3 G major...and its relative minor

You've already learned the scale of C major – all the white keys from C to C. But what happens if you want to play a scale of G major? If you play all the white keys from G to G, one of the notes sounds wrong – try it! Which note sounds wrong? To get the special pattern of tones and semitones in a major scale, you need an F sharp.

The sharp sign (♯) raises the pitch of a note by a semitone.

So, pieces in the key of G major start like this:

It's a **key signature**.

The sharp symbol (♯) is placed on the F line. It reminds you that you must play every F as an F sharp.

Now practise the right-hand G major scale a few times.
The fingering is the same as for the C major scale.

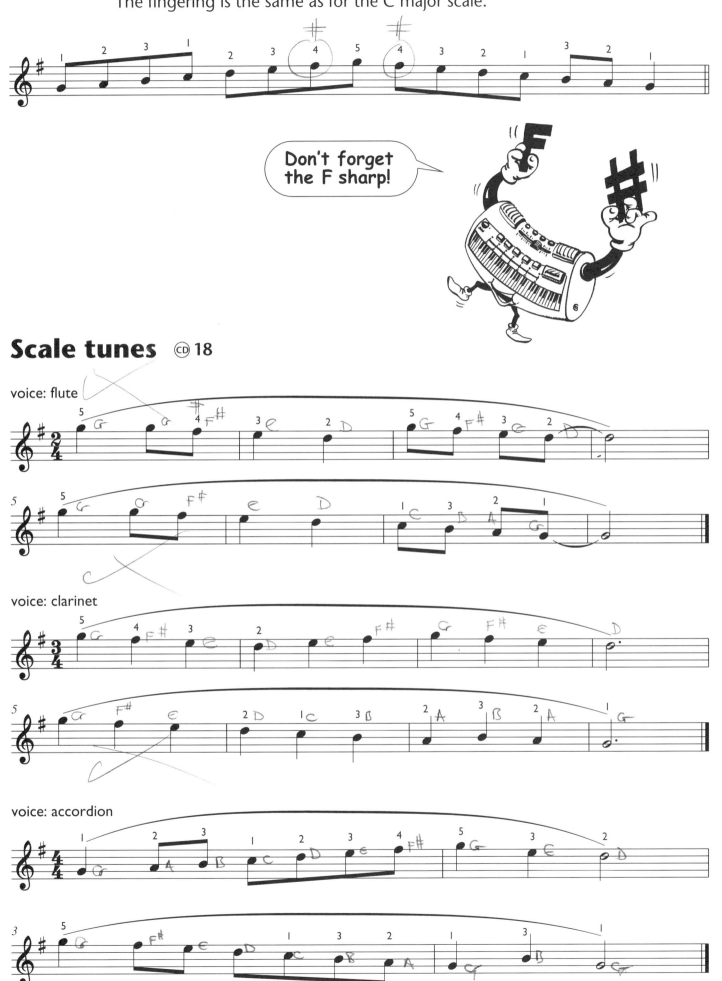

Scale tunes CD 18

voice: flute

voice: clarinet

voice: accordion

Three useful chords in G major

chord I = G; chord IV = C; and chord V = D.

Vespers CD 19

voice: strings
style: bass chord hold

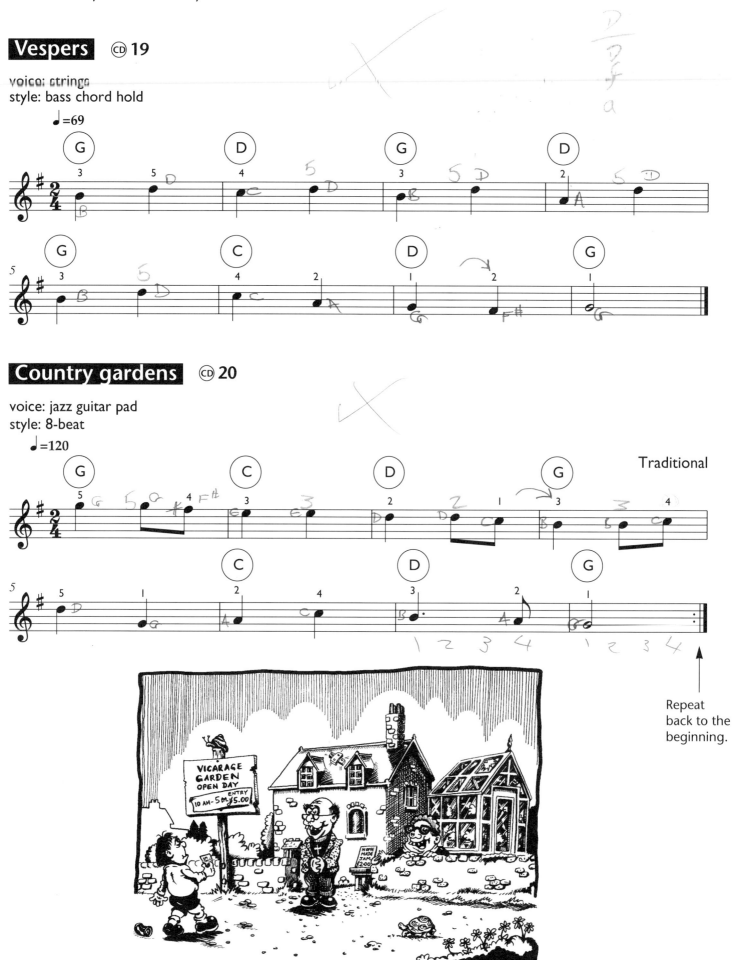

Country gardens CD 20

voice: jazz guitar pad
style: 8-beat

Traditional

Repeat
back to the
beginning.

Now try the same pieces in the key of C major. Notice how chords I, IV and V are now C, F and G.

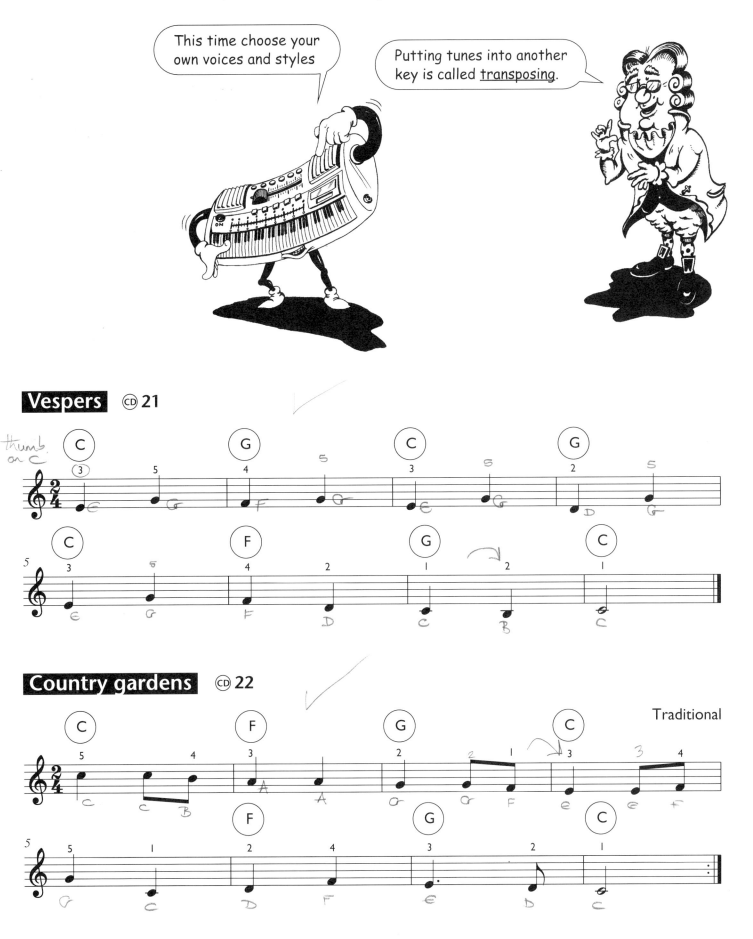

Vespers ⓒ**21**

Country gardens ⓒ**22**

Traditional

More bass clef notes

Make sure the auto-accompaniment is switched off for these melodies.

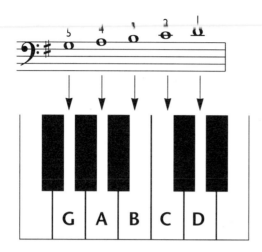

Left-hand solo melodies

Solemn solo ⓒⒹ 23

voice: electric bass

Slinky solo

voice: sustained strings

Syncopated solo

voice: tenor saxophone

Hands together

Practise each hand separately first.

Octave rock no. 1   CD 24

voice: electric guitar

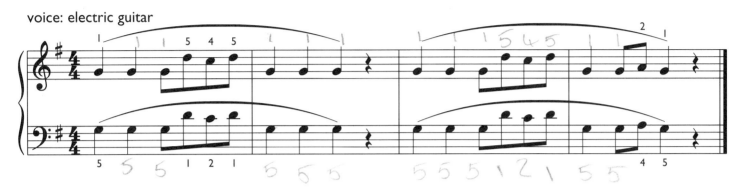

Octave rock no. 2

voice: electric guitar

Lilting lullaby   CD 25

voice: sustained harp

Echo games CD 26

Listen to these simple phrases played by
your teacher, then play them back. No
looking at the music! The notes are all
between G and D in the treble clef.
Stick to your G major 5-finger position.
Good luck!

Teachers' instructions

You will need at least two keyboards: one for
yourself and one for each student. Check that the
students stick to the G major 5-finger position,
and give them as many chances as they need to
repeat each phrase correctly. Change the rhythmic
style accompaniment from time to time to give
variety.

Teachers' note

If there isn't time for **Echo games** in
the lesson, ask the students to use the
material for sight-reading practice.

Let's rumba! ⓒ**27**

voice: vibes
style: rhumba

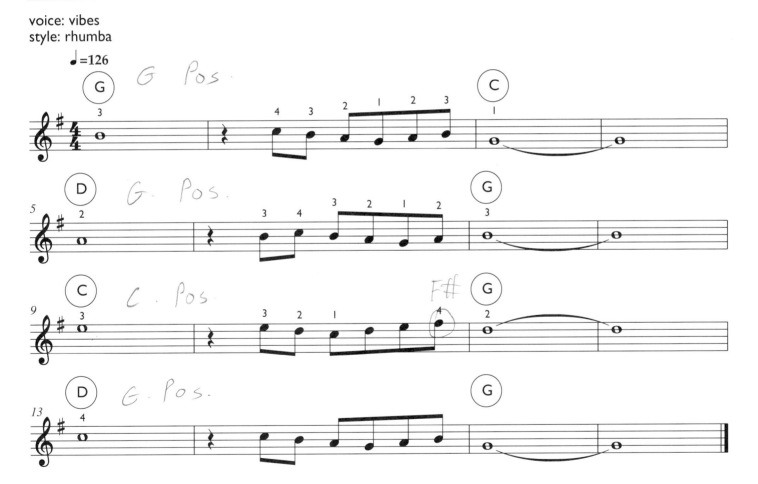

A rumba (or rhumba) is a Cuban dance
with an African flavour. The music has a
syncopated beat and the dance is very
complicated!

The TV detective CD **28**

A mysterious theme to suit the character of a dynamic super-sleuth! E minor (Em), the relative minor of G major, is introduced here. Like G major, E minor also has a single sharp in its key signature.

voice: clavi/electric guitar
style: dance funk

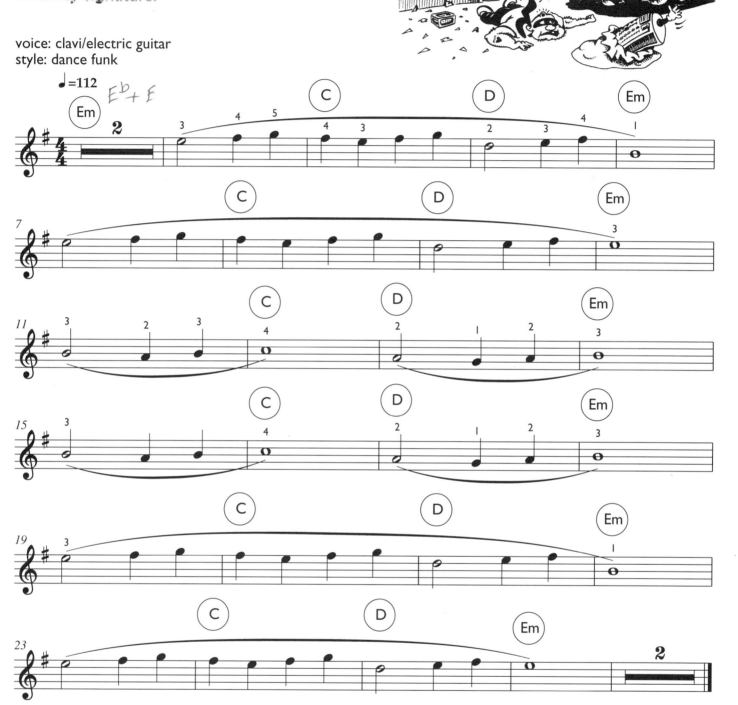

Do you remember how to play a minor chord using auto-accompaniment? Press the keynote and the next black key down for Yamaha keyboards, and on Casio keyboards the keynote and the next white note to the right.

F major...and its relative minor

That's a scale of F major. The key signature is one flat – B flat. How do you find B flat on the keyboard?

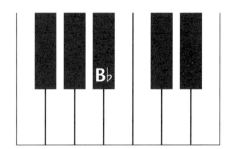

The flat sign (♭) lowers the pitch of a note by a semitone.

Now practise the right-hand F major scale a few times.
Notice how 5th finger isn't used – even at the top!

thumb under

4th finger over thumb

Don't forget the B flat!

Solo melodies using the scale of F major

Dotty solo 🄯 29

voice: piano

finger over

Graceful solo

voice: strings

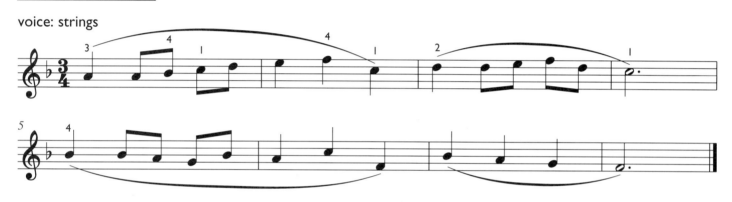

Forthright solo

voice: saxophone

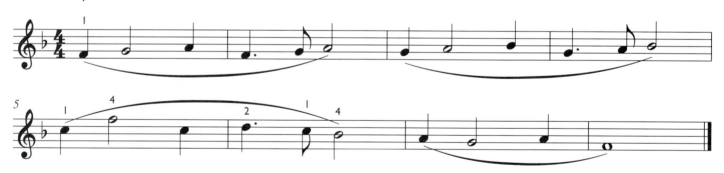

GROUPS Provide a percussion accompaniment to the solo player, in the manner of *Drumkit Dynamo* on page 13 (using a high sound and a low sound). If there are any real percussion instruments handy you could use them.

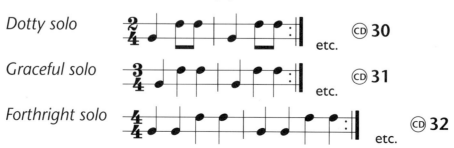

Dotty solo   etc.   🄯 **30**

Graceful solo   etc.   🄯 **31**

Forthright solo   etc.   🄯 **32**

Three useful chords in F major
chord I = F; chord IV = B♭; chord V = C.

Home on the range ⓒⒹ 33

voice: violin country/harmonica
style: waltz

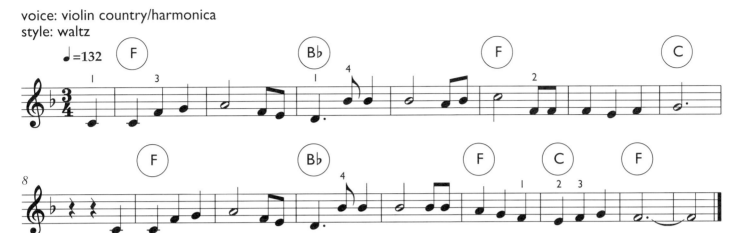

Dotted quavers (dotted eighth notes)

In the next piece, each beat has a dotted quaver plus a semiquaver (sixteenth note) – so keep the rhythm crisp.

count: one - i - and - a

If you're happy and you know it ⓒⒹ 34

voice: clarinet trio/electric piano
style: rock shuffle

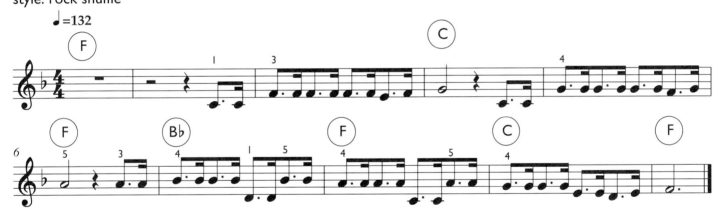

Transposition ⓒⒹ 35

Here's the tune of *Home on the range* transposed into G major.
See if you can play it and work out the chords yourself.

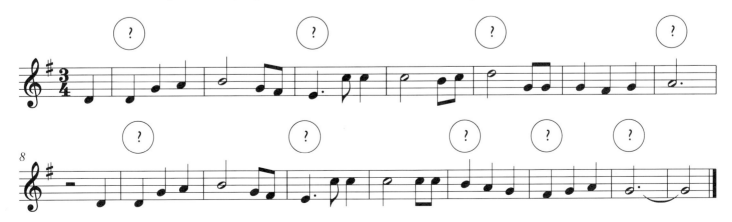

More bass clef notes

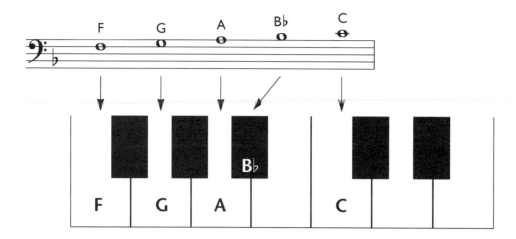

Left-hand solo melodies

Little march   CD 36

voice: trombone

Winsome waltz

voice: electric bass

Brisking along

voice: marimba

GROUPS Play along using the same
notes but an octave (eight notes) higher.

Hands together

Both hands stay in the F major 5-finger position.

Octave funk no. 1   ⓒ 37

voice: electric guitar

♩=120

Octave funk no. 2

voice: electric guitar

♩=120

Like all funk music, these tunes involve lots of syncopation! Clap and count them before you try them on the keyboard.

Bach's musette   ⓒ 38

voice: harpsichord/piano

Allegretto ♩=88

Polonaise ⓒ 39

A polonaise is a national dance of Poland, in triple
time, with a strong rhythmic flavour. Chopin wrote
many pieces in this style, and so did earlier composers
such as Bach and Handel. The example here is in a
baroque style (17th – early 18th centuries).

Using a percussion sound, practise these rhythms
before you start working on the piece. Use 2nd finger,
right hand.

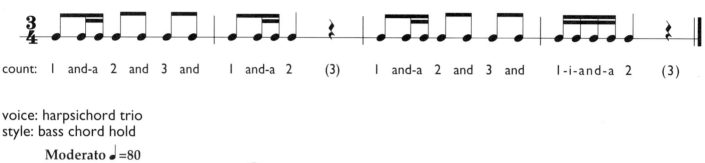

count: l and-a 2 and 3 and   l and-a 2   (3)   l and-a 2 and 3 and   l-i-and-a 2   (3)

voice: harpsichord trio
style: bass chord hold

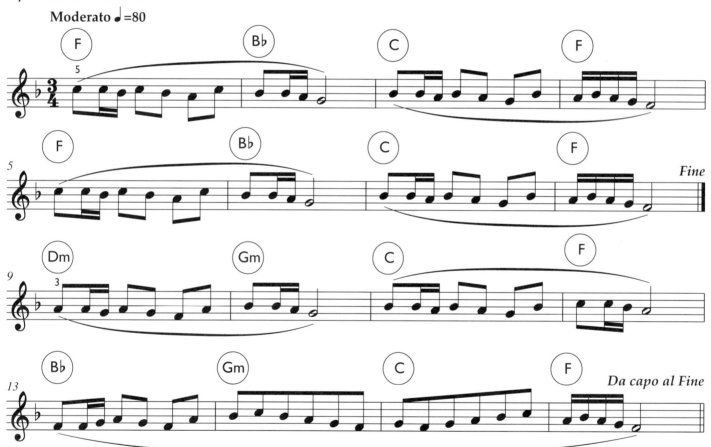

ⓒ 40 **GROUPS** One player could play the chords and
another the melody. A third player, or the teacher,
could add a percussion accompaniment using a sound
such as snare drum, repeating this rhythmic pattern:

l 2 3   l and-a 2 and 3

New chords

All the chords you've learned use the 1st, 3rd and 5th notes of the scale, sounding together. These exercises introduce a new type of chord – the 7th chord. 7th chords use the 1st, 3rd, 5th and flattened 7th notes of the scale for a really 'crunchy' effect! You can add a seventh to a major or minor chord. Here's how to play seventh chords. The examples shown are in D and A.

Yamaha

✖ ✖ = 7th chord

✖ ✖ (with ⊗ above) = Minor 7th chord

Casio

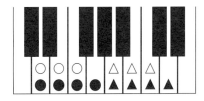

○ ○ ○ = D⁷ chord

● ● ● ● = Dm⁷ chord

△ △ △ = A⁷ chord

▲ ▲ ▲ ▲ = Am⁷ chord

Chord-changing exercises CD 41

style: eurobeat

♩=108

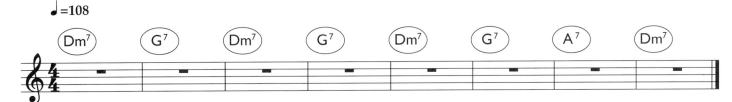

Dm⁷ G⁷ Dm⁷ G⁷ Dm⁷ G⁷ A⁷ Dm⁷

style: waltz

♩=120

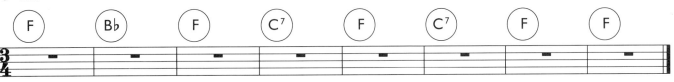

F B♭ F C⁷ F C⁷ F F

Chords 'n' tunes CD 42

voice: vibes
style: jazz latin

♩=104

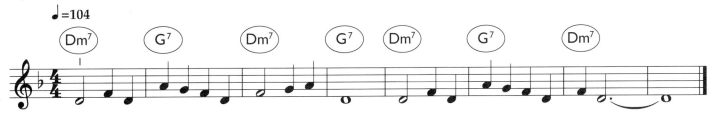

Dm⁷ G⁷ Dm⁷ G⁷ Dm⁷ G⁷ Dm⁷

voice: brass ensemble
style: R & B

♩=132

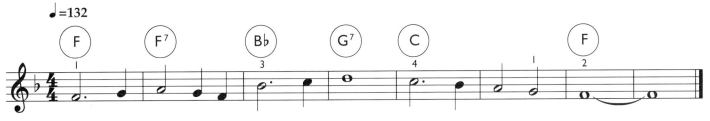

F F⁷ B♭ G⁷ C F

35

Groundbeat adventure CD 43

A funky number in D minor – the relative minor of F major.

This piece has just five notes in the right hand but quite a few chord changes! Practise with hands separately at first.

voice: vibraphone
style: groundbeat

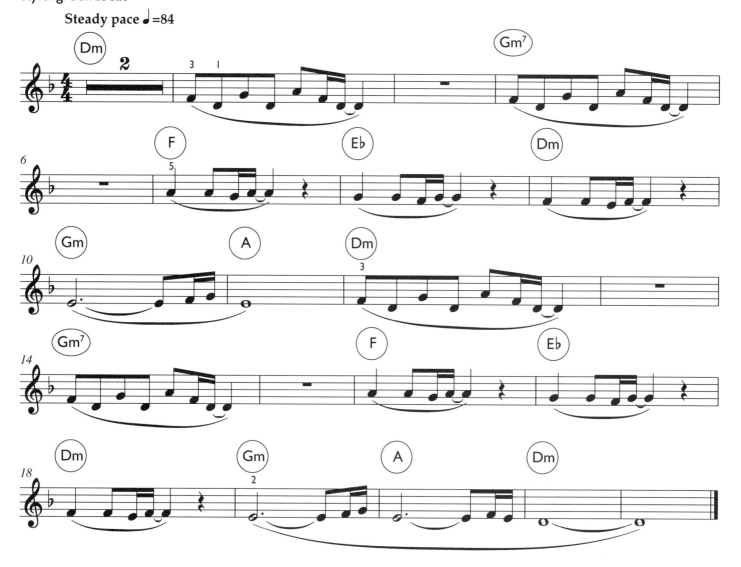

GROUPS CD 44

Player 1: melody
Player 2: chords
Other players: experiment with these rhythms, using an electronic percussion voice or real percussion instruments.

Now you know about:
- F major and its scale
- Flats
- Dotted quavers (dotted eighth notes)
- Seventh chords

unit 5 The blues   (CD) 45

The Blues is one of the most enduring and influential forms of popular music, originating amongst Afro-American people in the deep Southern States of the USA. As a musical form, it often features a 12-bar structure using chords I, IV and V.

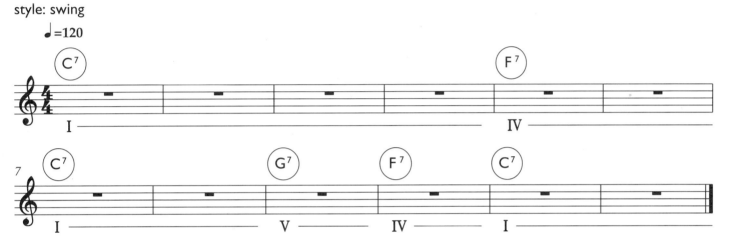

Now try playing the 12-bar blues in the key of G:

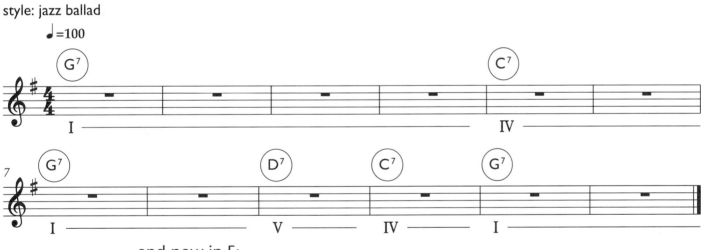

. . . and now in F:

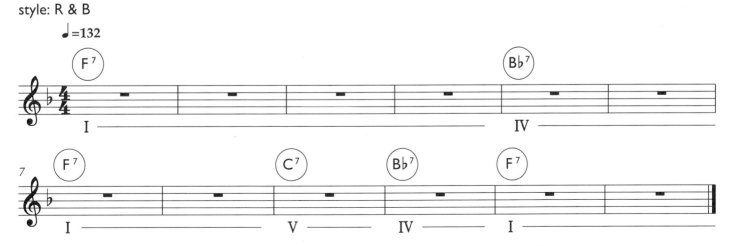

Drumkit dynamo no. 2   CD 46

The Blues often have a 'swinging' rhythmic style. This
means that crotchet beats (quarter notes) are divided
into three quavers (eighth notes), not two. Like this:

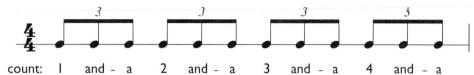

These groups of three are called triplets (indicated by *3*).
Try these rhythms using a high percussion sound in your
right hand and a low percussion sound in your left hand.

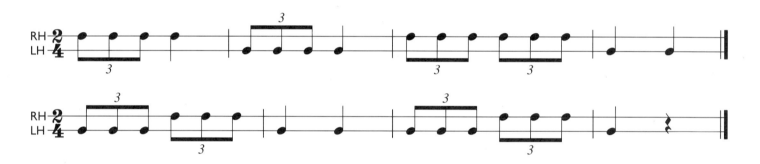

Now try these rhythms, where some of the crotchet beats
contain only two notes, a long one and a short one.

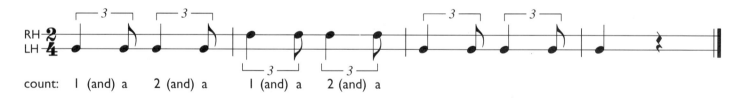

To make these rhythms easier to read, they are often

written out like this   [music]   etc. . . . . . .

with the following at the top of the piece: [music]

If you're playing a swing-style piece you'd
automatically play them in the style you've learned –
with the first note longer than the second. Try these:

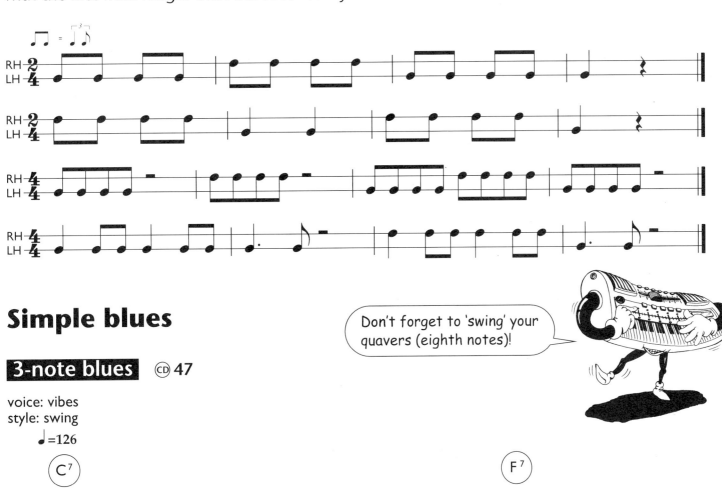

Simple blues

Don't forget to 'swing' your
quavers (eighth notes)!

3-note blues CD 47

voice: vibes
style: swing
♩=126

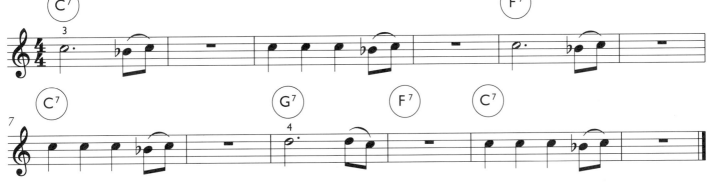

4-note blues CD 48

voice: electric piano
style: swing
♩=112

Did you notice that **3-note blues** uses B flat in its melody, even though it's in the key of C? That's because the blues often uses a different scale to the major scale. Here's a blues scale in C:

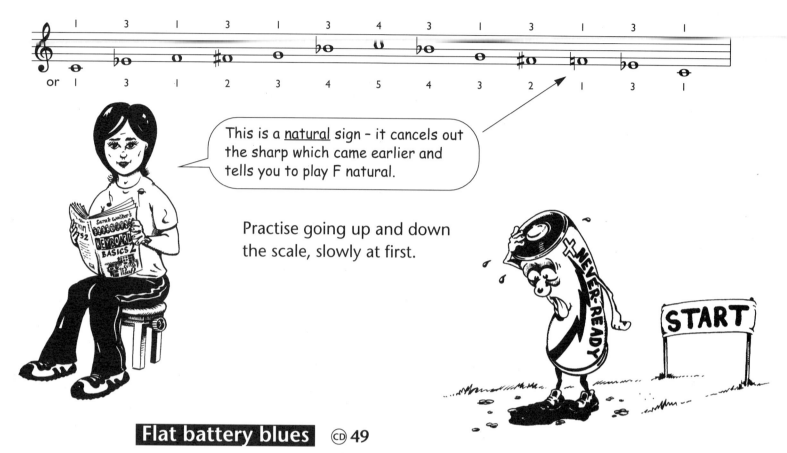

This is a <u>natural</u> sign – it cancels out the sharp which came earlier and tells you to play F natural.

Practise going up and down the scale, slowly at first.

Flat battery blues 　CD 49

A 12-bar blues which uses all the notes of the blues scale.

voice: vibes
style: swing

♩=116

* the B♭ earlier in the bar means that this B is flattened too.

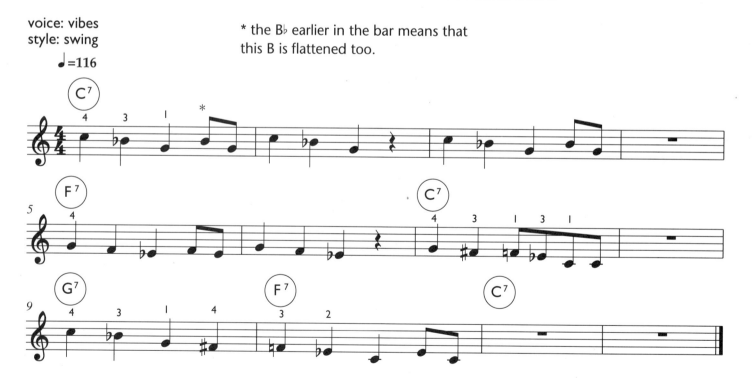

Blue cat blues ⓒⒹ 50

A rhythmic blues tune. If you find it hard to play
two notes at the same time in your right hand,
practise the tune without the top Cs and Ds.
The fingering works out just the same.

voice: piano
style: swing

♩=132

Blues improvisation no. 1 ⓒⒹ 51

Using notes from the blues scale in C, improvise your
own answering phrases:

continue:

Blues improvisation no. 2

continue:

Remember: the tune will only
feel 'finished' if you end on
the home-note, C.

Blues improvisation no. 3   CD 52

Now improvise in the gaps in this 12-bar blues.

voice: electric piano
style: swing

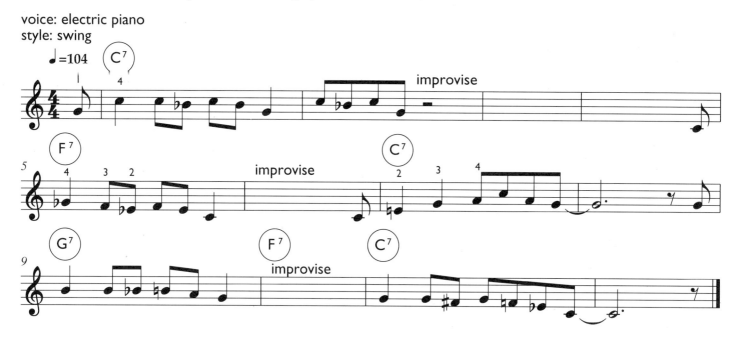

When you're confident with the chords, and have thought up some convincing melodic fills, try playing through the 12-bar blues progression improvising the entire right-hand part. Don't try to use all notes of the scale at once! Remember, you can make a blues from just three or four notes. And use plenty of rhythmic repetition.

GROUPS

Improvise a 12-bar blues together. It helps if you have a copy of the blues scale and chords to look at.

Player 1: autochords
Player 2: improvise the first four bars of the blues using a small selection of notes
Player 3: improvise the next four bars, continuing Player 2's idea
Player 4, or 2 again: complete the sequence

C Minor blues   CD 53

Change the tonic chord (chord I) into a minor chord and you get a different kind of blues – even cooler!

voice: chorus electric piano
style: swing

♩=116

Ultramarine blues   ⓒⅅ 54

. . . a blues in the key of G

voice: piccolo
style: swing

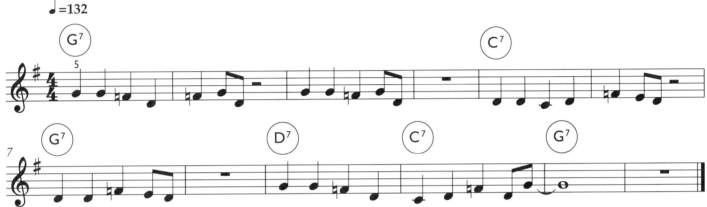

Aquamarine blues   ⓒⅅ 55

. . . a blues in the key of F

voice: fantasy 1
style: waltz/jazz waltz

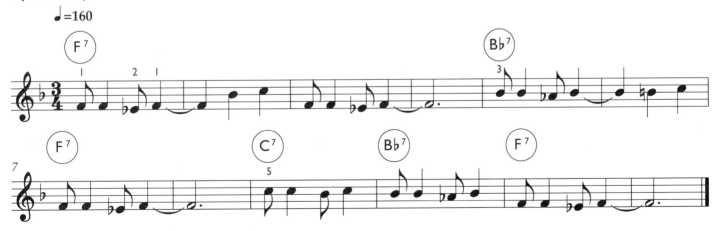

Clap and count this syncopated rhythm
before you start!

Now you know about:

- The 12-bar blues
- Triplets
- Swinging quavers
  (eighth notes)
- The blues scale
- Natural signs

Finishing touches

You'll never sound like a professional if you just plonk the notes down any-old-how. To give your playing finesse, you must think about articulation – *legato*, *staccato* and slurs.

Legato

Legato means playing smoothly – not letting go of one key before you put down the next. Try to pass smoothly from right hand to left hand without a break. The curved lines above and below the notes are phrase marks – think of a phrase as a musical sentence.

Sail on, little boat   CD 56

voice: pan flute

Moderato ♩=126

Traditional Chinese

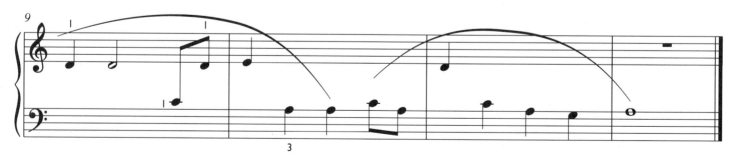

CD 57
by groups

GROUPS Using a soft voice, accompany the melody by repeating this pattern of chords. Another player could provide a drone by playing a low sustained A throughout.

Skye boat song CD 58

This popular Scottish song is based on a sea shanty. Play as smoothly as you can.

voice: folk guitar
style: bass chord hold

Staccato

Staccato notes are marked with a dot. They are very short and detached – the opposite of *legato*. In this exercise, left hand imitates right exactly – that's called a **canon**.

c stands for common time, or $\frac{4}{4}$ time.

Staccato canon   CD 59

What shall we do with the drunken sailor?   CD 60

voice: accordion

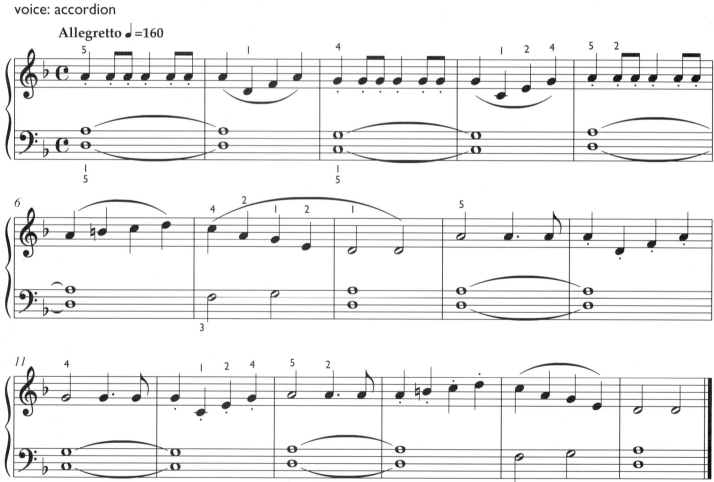

CD 61   **GROUPS** Using a percussion voice or real percussion instruments (tambourines would work well), additional players could add the following part:

46

Slurs

A curved line connecting two or more different notes is called a slur. Like a phrase mark, it means you must join the notes smoothly, but try to shade off on the last note of the group. Try this right-hand exercise:

> Your hand should bounce up slightly on the last note of each group.

Lightly row · ⓒ 62

voice: flute
style: bossa nova

The keel row · ⓒ 63

voice: folk guitar pad
style: 8–beat

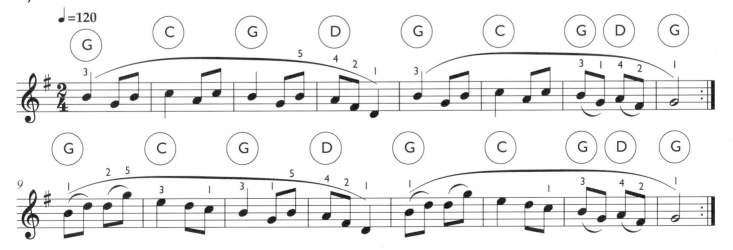

Grace notes

When playing many kinds of popular music, a keyboard player will often decorate the melodic line with grace notes, or crushed notes. These notes are very short, and slide quickly on to the main melodic note.

Try this right hand exercise:

Grace note exercise ⓒ**64**

Here's another exercise to help you with the moving parts in **Ben's ballad**. Watch the fingering!

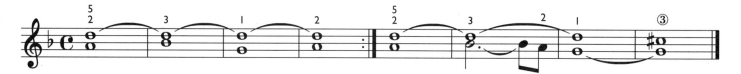

Ben's ballad  CD 65

voice: electric piano pad/electric piano
style: soul ballad

Fairly slow ♩=88

Now you know about:

- *Legato*
- *Staccato*
- Slurs
- Grace notes
- Common time

unit 7 Building a repertoire

You should always have a few simple pieces ready to perform for when you are asked to play in class or at home.

Go back through this book now, or through *Electronic Keyboard Basics 1*, and list ten pieces that you really enjoy playing. They could be simple exercises or longer pieces.

My repertoire

Name of piece   *Memorized?*

1 _____ ☐
2 _____ ☐
3 _____ ☐
4 _____ ☐
5 _____ ☐
6 _____ ☐
7 _____ ☐
8 _____ ☐
9 _____ ☐
10 _____ ☐

Now practise these pieces until you know them off by heart. Tick the box when you're confident they're memorized. You should be ready to play music from your repertoire whenever you are asked – get your teacher to test you each week! If you have a group lesson, perform pieces to your fellow students.

Concert performance

Have at least one piece in your repertoire which is suitable for playing in a concert. Any of the three pieces in this unit would be ideal if you are asked to play in public. Here are some handy hints:

1 Check the keyboard is working and select the correct voice, style and volume before you start.

2 Take your time adjusting the stool so it's the right height for you, and is facing the centre of the keyboard (if you're standing, check that the keyboard itself is at a sensible height). Don't be afraid to make your audience wait – it'll be worth it in the end!

3 Don't drop your hands away from the keyboard the second you've finished playing! Switch off the rhythm (if necessary); pause with your hands above the keys for a moment and finally lower your hands decisively as if to say 'You may clap now!'

4 Give a small bow to acknowledge the applause.

Deep river CD 66

This well-known spiritual, or religious folksong was first sung by the Afro-American slaves in the Deep South in the 19th century.

voice: strings
style: pop ballad

Fairly slow ♩=84

Traditional

GROUPS Divide into melody players and chord players. For the first few run-throughs, use bass chord hold instead of a rhythmic style.

Wolsey's Wilde CD 67

A traditional tune named
after Henry VIII's famous
adviser Cardinal Wolsey.

voice: harpsichord

Traditional

If the low B♭ in bar 36 is out of your keyboard range, just play F.

68 **GROUPS** Using a percussion voice or real drums, extra players could add this accompaniment. Or play the melody along with player 1, using a strong melodic voice such as oboe.

This is a **mordent** – a small trill. Play it like this: Can you find any other places where a mordent might sound effective?

Walking in the air ⓒ 69

from *The Snowman*

voice: sustained vibraphone
style: pop ballad

Steady pace ♩=88

Howard Blake

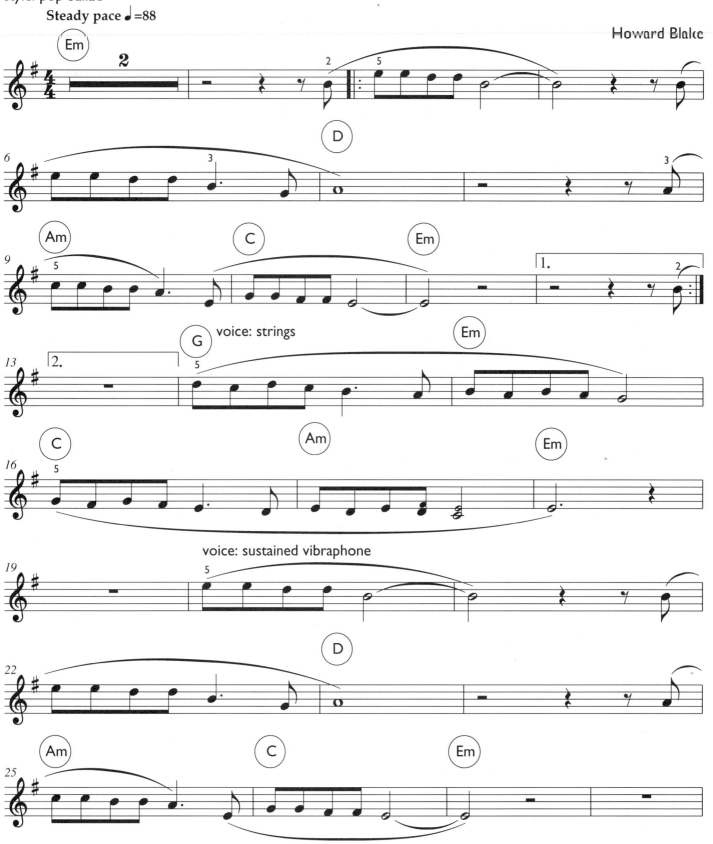

voice: strings

voice: sustained vibraphone

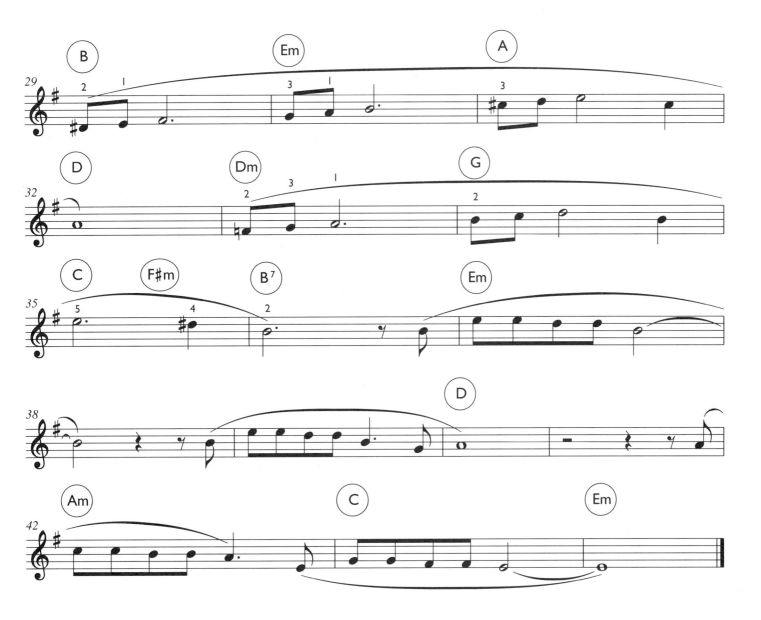

Make sure you are able to reprogramme the voices quickly in bars 14 and 20! If you run out of time, wait for another whole bar before continuing with the melody.

GROUPS Perform to each other and offer constructive suggestions: was the tempo too fast or too slow? Which parts needed more practice, and why? Which parts were most successful? Do you have any suggestions to make regarding fingering?

Now you know about:

- Building a repertoire
- Performing skills
- Mordents

Glossary

Auto-accompaniment function splits the keyboard into upper (melody) and lower (auto-accompaniment). The point of this division is marked above the keyboard.

Chord symbols are given above the musical stave, and should be followed both for 'single-fingered' and 'fingered' chords. Where chord symbols are used in this book you should play the same chord until the symbol changes.

Fingered chords give the same effect as 'single-fingered', but are achieved by pressing down a whole triad (the three notes which make up the chord).

Single-fingered chords allow you to play a chord by pressing one or two keys in the auto-accompaniment range of your keyboard. For a major chord play one note and for a minor two notes, depending on the make of your keyboard.

Start/Stop button enables rhythm to be started or stopped.

Style e.g. *samba*, enables the player to choose from a wide range of settings that include rhythm accompaniment plus a compatible 'voice' (see below).

Synchro. start enables the rhythm to start by pressing any note in the 'auto-accompaniment' section of the keyboard. Once a 'style' is selected that section will standby until the note is pressed.

Voice gives the player a choice of instrumental sound, e.g. *trumpet* or *electric piano*.

To buy Faber Music publications or to find out about the full range of titles available please contact your local music retailer or Faber Music sales enquiries:
E-mail: sales@fabermusic.co.uk
Website:http://www.fabermusic.co.uk